HEMMING FLAMES

May Swenson
Poetry Award Series
Volume 19

HEMMING FLAMES

poems
by

Patricia Colleen Murphy

UTAH STATE UNIVERSITY PRESS
Logan

Published by Utah State University Press
An imprint of University Press of Colorado
5589 Arapahoe Avenue, Suite 206C
Boulder, Colorado 80303

 The University Press of Colorado is a proud member of
the Association of American University Presses.

The University Press of Colorado is a cooperative publishing enterprise supported, in part,
by Adams State University, Colorado State University, Fort Lewis College, Metropolitan
State University of Denver, Regis University, University of Colorado, University of Northern
Colorado, Utah State University, and Western State Colorado University.

∞ The paper used in this publication meets the minimum requirements of the American
National Standard for Information Sciences—Permanence of Paper for Printed Library
Materials. ANSI Z39.48-1992

ISBN: 978-1-60732-551-2 (cloth)
ISBN: 978-1-60732-557-4 (paperback)
ISBN: 978-1-60732-552-9 (ebook)
DOI: 10.7330/9781607325229

Library of Congress Cataloging-in-Publication Data
Names: Murphy, Patricia Colleen, 1970– author. | Dunn, Stephen, 1939– writer of foreword.
Title: Hemming flames : poems / by Patricia Colleen Murphy.
Other titles: May Swenson Poetry Award series ; v. 19.
Description: Logan : Utah State University Press, [2016] | Series: May Swenson Poetry Award
    series ; volume 19
Identifiers: LCCN 2016008373| ISBN 9781607325512 (cloth) | ISBN 9781607325574
    (pbk.) | ISBN 9781607325529 (ebook)
Classification: LCC PS3613.U7528 A6 2016 | DDC 811/.6—dc23
LC record available at http://lccn.loc.gov/2016008373

Cover series design by Barbara Yale-Read
Cover art: "Con i denti," by Elisa Talentino

for John

CONTENTS

FOREWORD

The curious title of Patricia Murphy's wonderfully disturbing *Hemming Flames* doesn't become clear to us until the last poem in the book. And, as good titles do, it provides a way of understanding what have been the book's necessities and, in this case, its tonal harshness. The last two lines are, "Yesterday I invented fire. / Today I'm hemming flames." The "today" stands for almost every poem Murphy artfully offers us, as if the act of writing these poems was an attempt to hem what can't easily be hemmed. Or maybe to think of the paradoxical nature of the title is more instructive. Flames can be extinguished, but can they be hemmed? Perhaps one can only try. Poem after poem delivers a dysfunctional family—father, mother, brother, the speaker herself—with only the slightest redemption in sight. There's a Plathian relentlessness to the book. And, like Plath, Murphy never forgets that she's writing poetry as she indicts ("They would have given us / absolutely everything / they didn't want.") And there's just enough well-phrased complicity in the telling to make us trust the speaker. She wonders, "What if today, I touch everyone I see. / I'm not afraid to hit someone if they need it." And in one of the many poems addressed to the mother, we are told, "I have promised others I will never / want the way you want. / They love me on this condition."

Though some might worry that the book can at times seem to be a tell-all, I never felt that the motive behind it was therapeutic. Patricia Murphy is a maker of poems. If the slight redemption I mentioned above exists, it is in the way we, the readers, are made privy to an ever-expanding consciousness. She knows what she feels, and has felt. But she writes, like the best of writers do, to find the language for what she thinks.

Stephen Dunn

LOSING OUR MILK TEETH

Back then we were all such
good little Bolsheviks.

Now I am that vaguely
familiar character from

a film you cannot name.
What choice did I have

but to disappear from your
house of faulty methods?

You made sure I found you
so you could leave me

with my new name,
accomplice. And so we will

gather for one last parody
of a holiday. Dad will be all

smiles. He'll say, *pass the mother
fucking peas.* And, *could you*

*try not to murder yourself
in front of the children.*

BRIDGES ALL OVER THE ROOM

I've   known   my   mother
since   she   fell   in   love
with   the   on-call   oncologist.
I   remember   she   liked
to   read   shit   novels
over   strangers'   shoulders
on   the   airplane.   She
learned   to   name objects
by   scent: *citrus, musk.*
She   called   her   pockets   slotlets.
She   thought   all   ninjas were   chicks.
She   used   to   tell   me
I   was   strong   like
it   was   an   order.
Now   she's   in   bed   for
what   might   last   my   lifetime.
She   asked   for   political   asylum
in   the   lunatic   asylum.
I   begged   her   not
to   think   like   Berryman
since   there   are   bridges
all   over   the   room.

MY BROTHER, HOARDING

Now he wants wooden gloves
with ornate carvings of egrets,

detailed cuffs accentuating
the coquettishness of wrist skin.

Now he wakes to darkness
and so he yells, *water, water.*

In comes a shadow
and so he yells, *light.*

Now he is tired.
He secures his long hair

at the nape with a pencil,
a chopstick, or a spoon.

Now he is over 400
lbs and must be

taken to the cattle
ranch for weighing.

Now he phones to say *fire.*
It's as close as we've ever been.

He in my ear,
me in his.

HOW THE BODY MOVES

Melanie, the Siamese,
on the front porch with baby me.
In pictures, the two of us
are almost the same size.
Later my mother
bought Persians, bred them,
used the money for jewelry,
cigarettes, Drambouie.
The first time a litter came
she sent me searching the house
to find and clean the afterbirth.
I found the babies limp,
smothered in their sleep.

Only twenty more miles.
I am 15. My uncle is driving.
My mother has fled again in her
Oldsmobile, heading for Palo Alto.
We were fighting. She took
all the pills she could find.

My uncle sighs, repeats that
his mother died giving birth to him.
One tenth her weight, he came
screaming from her pelvis on the
coldest Minnesota day in history.

The freeway slips under us like night.
From here I think the hills are
impoverished sisters huddled for warmth
under green mohair blankets.
Seventeen of them: stomach to knee,
buttock to backbone.
We glide past their ankles.

Once I dreamt I was nine months pregnant.
When I went to the bathroom
the baby slipped out like a miraculous

bowel movement. She had blond hair,
and a T-shirt that said *French Countryside*.
A neighbor saw the birth through the window.
He smiled, continued mowing the back field,
and I hung a bell.

We loved the thrill of being batshit in a speedboat.
We wore our poison ivy like tattoos. There wasn't
much positive feedback. We'd go to the dock to fish
for catcalls. Brother, we were nearly twins in our red
swimming bottoms. In the evenings we mixed
martinis, always caring for our parents just short
of paying the mortgage. Mornings, doughnuts
at an empty table. We were so small, but so adept
at pretending we weren't living with orangutans.
In August we'd leave the lake and return to the river.
All those winters spent in the throw-things house.
Ceramic ashtray exploding against brown paneling.
My head crashing through the china cabinet glass.
I knew exactly why you needed to touch me that way.

XVIIIE ARRONDISSEMENT

I was 15, sulking in the tub
of a bourgeois hotel room.

I heard her fighting her suitcase,
you mother-fucking cocksucker,

3 boxes of thigh-highs, 50 blank
cassette tapes, 5 cartons of cigarettes,

but no passports, since she had lost them,
claiming they were stolen by an Algerian

near the Centre Pompidou. Mother in her
white shirt and pants. The concierge

called to say stop drying your lingerie
in the window. Mother in her tiny white

sneakers. At the Sacre Coeur she asked
a man in a Kangol hat to uncork the bottle

of wine she swigged from, then shoved
at me. How did we make it back to Ohio?

I have spent so long apprenticed
to the drunk and insane

that I know terror dressing
up in anger's hat and coat.

Terror wearing anger's
fake mustache.

IMMOLATE

January. The snow's

      finally up to

           the cat's   belly.

Good little   stalker.

You're   swaddled   in   a

pink   snowsuit.   Knit   mittens.

Look at   your smile!

      One more like that, please.

And later we will

         drive across

             the bridge.

And later

      you will

         climb into

           my lap.

      That slight weight of you?

      A drug.

         Your baby body

back where it should be.

We'll blink and it's July.

         You're getting grown.

Your heavy breasts.   Your heavy breasts.

         Where did they come from!

         No one in my family had them!

Who fed you bagels?   I did not feed you bagels!

         It's hot as ass.

I will drive

    across the

        bridge.

On the other side

        my lap

           will be

a

    perfect place

        for gasoline.

CUTLASS CIERA

Of the attempts, I resent most not the one
that I myself derailed when I walked

in on you corpse-napping away an afternoon.
And how could I hate you for the ones I wasn't

even born for? Though I do. How you tried
to taste volts the day my brother was born.

The one that's hardest to forgive is that burning
Oldsmobile, the Sheriff who nearly died saving

you, the skin grafts, the methodone. Why?
I bet that day started with a sunrise.

I bet it started with you opening your eyes. I bet
it started with urination, medication, you shifting

the contents of the apartment where, you told me,
someone kept breaking in at night and mismatching

your closet full of shoes. I bet that day started with
a gas can. I've never known such certainty as you,

when you pulled into the spot where you meant
to die. Where you watered yourself like a little

daffodil—splash, splash, splash
across your roots.

KITTEN

We all drove our separate cars to probate court,
where we told the judge, biweekly, how much Mom
loved matches. Why didn't it occur to me to mention,
too, that every day when I came home from school
you were in the La-Z-Boy watching doubles, how
you'd stare at me then back at the screen and say
that when you saw the white mound under the short
skirt you felt like you could cum without even rubbing it.
When Dad returned from work he'd steal your throne.
Upstairs I'd conjugate French verbs, analyze infinitesimals,
mom's skin grafts floating in and out like red admirals.
Did you fanaticize about walking to the cliff with a sack
of women? Their fists and heels protruding like shifting
balls. The river so embarrassed to find itself wet.

MY ARMAMENTARIUM

Home was my favorite out of all the asylums.
Like being on a ship full of disgruntled Vikings.

I remember our mother feeding us malice from cans.
Our father walking around in extraordinary costumes.

It's true I'm the person who has been known to say
How can they afford all those children they're having.

That I'm the first in the car to shout *that is not my heroin*!
But let's have it out, brother. Since you're the one exclaiming

quelle époque. Talk to me of your failed pandemonium lessons.
Talk to me of spending all your money on Russian things.

How many people, in the end, can claim they were never loved?

IS IT THE SEA YOU HEAR IN ME?

In the kitchen my brother smashes jars
of Devon's Maraschino Cherries.

The glass cuts his fingers.
He likes the way the reds blend.

In the bathroom upstairs
I tell the water,

I am not afraid to touch you.
I want to see it shiver

so I drop a smile into the tub
near the edge. Irretrievable!

I lie down with a book
and begin to tear the pages.

My brother enters.
I want to play, he says.

I use the hem of my yellow
dress to brush away my tears.

He goes downstairs and drinks
from the kitchen faucet

and then he carves
sailboats into the linoleum.

I know I might become the book.
I know I might become the bed.

GOOD MORNING, MEDIOCRITY

I wake up again between the masturbator and the hoarder.

The boxes are labeled *Thai Tiles* as if there are any other kind.

The other boxes are labeled *snowflakes*, *groves*, *displeasures*.

I'd love nothing more than to drag them to Manila.

The masturbator must be a genius. I know this because

I'm young, yet I'm already tired of touching myself.

And the hoarder? Must be a ghost. I know this because

to manage, I've gotten rid of things that never existed.

It's a beautiful day outside. But I'm stuck between

the one who keeps it all and the one who gives it all away.

I think, but isn't the masturbator really a hoarder?

And isn't the hoarder really a masturbator?

Look at that turbulent sunrise. "Hooray for doom! Hooray!"

MEET THE AUTHOR

A 100-page binder held your arguments against abortion
written in tiny script. You were 16 years old. My best
friend was named Barbette and our matching stuffed dogs
had white ears. It was the summer of self-administered
mullets. Mom would stop at McDonald's for shakes
so she had something to swallow her Lithium with.
Of course you were right I was a fucking cunt. At night
I used my tongue to drop the needle onto the smooth
edge of every record. Of course you were right I was
a shameless slit. You saw my loose breasts floating like pears
in the deep end. Yes, I let him press against me in the pool,
his finger hooking the elastic hem of my bikini bottom.
Mother's cigarette shimmering in the kitchen window.

NIGHT FALLING, CZECHOSLOVAKIA

Drowsy over the cobbles
I pass a portrait of Kafka
chalked like a hallucination
on the wall of a preschool.
The day is turning pink.

On the subway a blond child rocks
with the swaying of the train. Soon
we have changed places. I am now
swaddled in the lap of a mother wearing
jewelry shaped like shucked oysters.

My stop trembles into view so I wade
in the whispers of the hookers
of Václavské náměstí, reaching the
square as the astronomical
clock clicks toward 7 p.m.

In the cloudy dining room of a hotel
I can't read the menu. I tap the woman
beside me. Pointing to the menu
I purse my lips like a fish and
she offers the English word "trout."

It arrives, has eyes bluer than mine and
scales of sparkling silver. I wish to pluck
them and present them to her like coins.
But she has disappeared. Among
all the faces in the street I can't find

the woman, the mother, or myself.
I am buying crepes from a stand near
the Church of St. Nicholas.
I am listening to jazz near Hradčany.
I am drinking beer at U Pinkasů.

I am looking for the child again,
the mother on the train.
I search for the woman in the din.

EDISON'S MEDICINE

How many blue volts before
Mom's in a better mood?

This time she took her tea
cups: Limoges, porcelain,

flecked with real gold! Her will
written in stark block letters

on yellow accountant's paper.
Zap! Her father's clarinet.

Zap! Her puppy Tar, black paws
folded over the Buick's back seat.

Zap! That night when my
father climbed a tree, sang

*I know a place where the music
is fine,* and did he? Did he?

They would have given us
absolutely anything

they didn't want.

I set fire to the gate because I am 69 years old and developers took
my property and did not fully compensate me. That made me very
angry. Afterwards I repeated that nobody got hurt. I repeated that
you can always restore cultural heritage. Now I'm in jail. Today I read
that 13-year-old Sameer Mishra from West Lafayette, Indiana spelled
guerdon correctly to win the 81st Scripps National Spelling Bee. The
Hart Crane poem *To Brooklyn Bridge* includes the word guerdon. James
Tate claimed that he read the poem *To Brooklyn Bridge* over 500 times.
Guerdon. The news reports said that winning the Bee was a guerdon.
In his poem Crane said, "Thy guerdon . . . Accolade thou dost bestow."
I wonder why Crane included the definition of the word in his poem,
as if he were writing it to be read at the Scripps National Spelling Bee?
He could have read the poem at the 5th Bee in 1932, but instead he
threw himself off the deck of a ship. To burn down the gate I took
a ladder to its base. I took some paint thinner, some lighters. After I
burned down the gate there was a lot of blame and a lot of sorrow. For
that I apologize. Mourners brought offerings: flowers, apples, pears,
persimmons, coffee beans, dried pollock, clams, bottles of soju and,
a grilled cheese sandwich. A child left this note to the gate: "It must
have been very hot while you were burning." My name is Chae Jong-gi
and now I am a poet but I used to be a fortune teller. In 2006 I burned
down Changgyeong palace, but that was a small fire and only caused
damage worth 4 million won. I apologized and I showed my sorrow
so the judge suspended my sentence. In 1957, his last year of eligibility
for the Bee, 14-year-old James Tate from Kansas City, Missouri could
have spelled schappe for a three way tie with Sandra Owen from
Canton, Ohio and Dana Bennett from Denver, Colorado. *Schappe*—to
remove silk waste by fermentation. Hart Crane from Garrettsville,
Ohio missed being eligible for the Bee by 13 years. Hardly enough to
suicide for, but look at that Bridge poem and you'll see he had a thing
for definitions. In 1956, at the age of 13, Tate could have won with
the word condominium. Think of all the condominiums in Brooklyn.
In Seoul we just call them apartments, which is easier to spell. My
name is Chae Jong-gi and I am only 5 years older than James Tate. If
I had been born in Dublin, Ohio or Lawrenceville, Indiana, in 1953 I
could have beaten Elizabeth Hess from Phoenix, Arizona by spelling

soubrette: a female servant or attendant, especially as mischievous or cheeky, often featured in theatrical comedies. But I was born in Goyang, Gyeonggi Province. *G.* Guerdon. If I were James Tate I might have burned down the St. Louis arch and if I were Hart Crane I might have burned down the Brooklyn Bridge. *U.* Guerdon. I burned down the gate because sometimes all that is left to do is jump off the back of a steamliner heading to a city with a big national landmark you once wrote a poem for. *E.* Guerdon, a reward, recompense. *R.* Guerdon, payment for services rendered. *D.* Guerdon, from Middle English, from Old French, Medieval Latin. *O.* Guerdon, accolade thou dost bestow. *N.* Guerdon. They took me back to the gate so I could show how I did it. The cameras were only a few feet from my face. I wore a mask so I would not shame my children. Guerdon, noun. Guerdon, no alternate pronunciations. Guerdon, Gate of Exalted Ceremonies. Guerdon, Great Southern Gate.

HIGH HOPES, BAD HABITS

I spend all day in a string
bikini, re-allocating

tan lines. The sun arches.
Then a moon chaser.

Here's what I will
accomplish: stay

awake. If awake, try not
to stare. If staring, stop.

Try to sturdy the two
fingers because they could

be new legs. I could tilt
up on them and walk away.

But I spend all day in a string
ball. I'm one in a pack

of javelina knocking over
the petunias. I'm the

pig in a two-piece.
Snorter.

TURKISH GET-UPS

I thought she meant costumes but she meant
what's inevitable when you're down. It is how

to stay exceptionally strong, she says. She says
this to me often out of one of her many mouths.

We're born prone, she says. *Then we roll onto
our bellies. Up*, she says. *Get up*, she says. *Get up.*

I am down and I hear her in the other room.
Without visual clues, I can't tell the exact

meaning of her statements. She says, *it is not
hyperbole if it is true.* She says, *you began life*

as a vowel. She says, *people incapable
of guilt can have a really great time.*

FEEDING PEEPING TOM

My mother's letters were all the same. She wrote,

Don't act so defeatist, dear. It's terribly middle class.

My Tom was always sideways. He might have been

missing an ear. He was off meat due to a brush with gout.

I made him vegan stews, mostly. And sweet potato pies.

I remember spring came quickly, dressed as an amputee.

More often than not when I looked out Tom was missing.

I wondered if he had ever even existed. My mother's letters

began to cover topics like giving coupons as gifts.

After my Tom left I never wrote to her again.

SCROTUM AND BONE

You learned to masturbate while I learned
to menstruate. How thin the wall separating
all our adolescent groaning. In our shared
bathroom, my obscene arsenal of hygienics.
In the hallway, a shelf of your hard-core porn.
Mom/Dad comatose in front of the TV, mistaking
money for generosity. Dysmenorrheaic, I rocked
in bed watching rabbits gnaw carrots on the wall.
I heard you blow your nose into a sock. We had
nowhere to go. Every so often, a source-less light
shone under our door cracks. There we were.
And the next day we were old.

*Dear Stylish Persons. I received your forms and the SHOCK
of your GOD-be-DAMNED diagnosis has made me change
my mind in a hurry. Sorry you SHIT HEADS! I'll fight this
to the US SUPREME COURT. Up Your Collective Assholes!*

What were the doctors doing with their pretty PhD's?
The rest of us cowered, studying for our turbulence exams.
Mom kept flashing her wallet open to her CPUSA card,
all while farting on the "Why don't you love me" cushions.

*Dear Honorable Sir. When I was an IRS auditor we targeted
migrant workers until I advised one of them to find a post-office
money-order receipt. Now the STATE of VIRGINIA PERSISTS
in HARRASSING me due to my radical religious & political beliefs.*

Dear Mother. To think that your hero, Sanger, argued
for forced sterilization in the asylums. No one could
accuse you of being feeble-minded, but let's discuss insane.
No summer ever came to you that did not wear a parka.

Brother whining, "It's a horrible day for my agoraphobia."
Why couldn't we ever coordinate our agony? Was I too
young or too old? Let's face it. I've never been the right age.
Think of the courage it took for me to touch a doorknob.

THE PRINCESS OF CREEPING

I remember I was staring at a water puppet.
That's not right. I was folding trumpets

into delicate triangles to give to the boys
who would take turns flicking them.

Or, I was braiding & unbraiding the silk
hair of the ear of corn the boys gave me.

I guess now's the time to admit
I don't precisely remember everything.

But I do know how it felt when the cat
kept slinking closer to the room

full of coyotes in costume. And even
though I let things nearly happen,

no one can say I did not live a long time
in the danger theater, where the play begins

with all the dolls behaving perfectly.

Palm leaves make me rustle, and gardenias.
I am using the pill to skip a period so I can swim
unplugged in the Andaman sea, and a man says
he loves me, but I can't tell where he is.

Anne is breaking down, a decade before my own Anne,
and for all the right reasons. Theirs are the days
of Thorazine, weight gain. At lunch by the beach
the man and I eat steaming Tom Yum Glang,

spicy as natives. We share Singhas while watching
the monsoon water attack itself with slapping.
The churning makes me crunch, clenches my jaw,
but the man says I am beautiful. *Was your Anne mad?*

I want to ask the man. *As mad as any Anne ever was?*
Did she pray for the rare days
her madness morphed into metaphor?
Did she seek altered states of (why does it) matter,

just like I've learned every good Anne should?
I don't tell the man over the Tom Yum that I'm contemplating
losing my mind. I let the helmeted hornbill chirp
from a tiled roof line. Later the man and I eat rambutan

as if it weren't ridiculous to do so. On the causeway
we dodge motorbikes, photograph the skinny fishes.
My period comes, spotting my polka dot bikini.
I've failed in my own annihilative way.

I turn some pages. I can't tell where Anne is.
And now where is the man? Where is the Andaman?
Catch me if you can. Anne is in the corner.
Anne falls down the stairs. Anne is in the bedroom.

Anne is on the chair. Anne pours out the whiskey.
Anne is in the shower. Anne applies her make-up.
Anne hikes to the tower. And a man calls my name.
Beautiful? He says. *Up for a swim?*

BULB

All I could do was take more late-night Olive
Garden shifts, adjust my maroon cummerbund
and hustle bottomless pasta. I parked my rusty
Mustang on the south-east pad of driveway, which
is how I got the name Prima Dona from you, forced
to street-park the K-car inherited from Mom after her
seventh asylum. Can you explain why we didn't speak
for 16 years? Your guinea pig named Jeremy was half
white and half brown. You liked to make sketches of
him in hats. I mistook his turd for a raisin but didn't
realize until I swallowed. How was I supposed to know
what to do about every pimply boy wanting to stick his
tongue in my mouth? If there were houses on our street
where that was not normal, I did not know them. Mom
thought your porn was a cute distraction. We always knew
what was coming when she started planting daffodils.

MURMUR

All the dog wants is to catch a baby bird
and then break her tiny neck and then

poke her pink brain with his pink tongue
and then spit out the feathers all over

the green ocean of the back lawn. Some
fucker on the radio is so right until he

is so wrong. Just ask mother, whose
last incarceration was a stick in the ass.

She said the Russian nurse sewed her anus
into a square. *A square?* I said. *A square,*

she said. I think of the kiosk at the mall
where the man tries to cover me in cuticle oil

every single time I pass by. I yell, *What is that
noise?* Always, the dog gnawing his own paw.

THE BIRTH OF NO

I remember everything but in an order I cannot control.

It was suicide season. I was 14 and I couldn't believe

my mother's thrift, like she had missed a few zeros.

It was in a room where everyone was known for something.

The doctor was wearing a double-breasted suit.

Later, I walked far away while pondering

What do I have to do to live to 15?

I passed that neighbor who was always doing something

ugly with his land. He asked me a question and when I

quoted Proust he asked, *Who is that? A family friend?*

Now the neighbor's fighting the hose. I keep counting

his trucks, thinking I am missing one.

What if, for today, I touch everyone I see?

I'm not afraid to hit someone if they need it.

MIDNIGHT AT ORCA CANNERY

Prince William Sound
I'm paddling an orange

kayak that must look
gray to the tenders

the tips of my paddle
disappear left right

rain clouds occluding
water seeping my skirt

the shore retreating
Sisyphus V. Poseidon

not sure if I'm afraid
to die or begging to.

Later in the cannery dorm
white walls and mattress

I wake sculling the ceiling
the water still mounts me

ticking strokes in the dark
whack at the dank buzz

of a trapped mosquito
in a white room like my

mother in a white room
just outside Moscow

a knock at the door
1 cold meal 1 Thorazine

lifting the robe again
the tips disappear

and what does breath offer?
only fog

LETTER FROM THE PSYCH WARD, HOSPITAL KASHENKO

Moscow, 1993

There's a Nigerian nurse here who reminds me of your first boyfriend,
black as carbon and big. Did you really think your father and I
couldn't hear you and that boy kissing on the living room floor
even when we found you mornings on the carpet,
your eggshell skin dwarfed by such muscle? Have you been
allowed to learn yet what I was taught at Bio I at Stanford
about the female ova being able to divide and form a fetus
on its own? The infant is always a girl or a hermaphrodite.
For heaven's sake, start saving each month's used tampons
and napkins in a cardboard box for shipment to Vat. City 2ND class,
surface "male" no return address for last *rights* and Holy
Internment because there is no way to know whether your ova
began dividing, forming a fetus which then miscarried.
The reason I asked you if you'd like me to buy you a Yugo
is that one of my daydreams in Moscow was for every family
with a teenager in the Industrialized World to put down money
on a Yugo so those ASSHOLE Yugoslavs would go back to work
instead of killing each other. I rode in a Yugo from the Rusky
Hotel Ukraine to the CIA Headquarters because at the time I thought
it was KGB Int'l. I walked into the secret entrance, asked for
protection as I was an American communist and Marxist
needing a safe place to stay. They disrobed me, drugged me,
drove me to the Hospital Kashenko (Cash & Go),
told the people at admitting such terrible lies about me.
The CIA agent was wearing a Halloween type fake walrus
mustache that covered most of his upper lip. He signed
his name "Jewryson" which, if you'll look up in your
"Holy Book," means son of all the Jews in the world.
My diet of eight sugar cubes (do wish Fidel would start planting
beets instead of cane) and three minute bowls of porridge
gave me a serious case of diabetes, so I telekenised my Salem 100's
into Naturales. Do you remember the Steve Ray Vaughn concert
I took you to with the two FBI agents sitting next to you
and the four kids in the seats in front of us smoking marijuana?

One of them offered me a drag and I said, "No thanks. It's illegal.
I'll just have another beer." Do you have a passport? When I get
out of here I will have enough money to take you with me
to Indonesia, where they sell Four Square, a medicinal herbal
cigarette that cures pulmonary disease. How is your asthma?
I begged your father not to smoke over the crib.

MY MITTELSCHMERZ

Her brothers preferred her locked up.
For 10 years we nearly lost track

of the asylums. In Ottawa
the Mounties had to charter

a bush plane to Thunder Bay Regional.
In Kingston lock-up, she demanded

that the rookie State Department agent
get Fidel on the phone and send a plane.

Still beautiful, still listing her return
address as the Russian Embassy.

And all that time I begged to not know.
So busy in the suburbs, growing

into my growing-into coat.

ARCH ON A RUNG
—with a line from Elizabeth Bishop's "Five Flights Up"

Bishop and I stay adamant our asthma
is NOT caused by our mothers' asylums.
Come on. I'm as bored of mom's suicides
as she is of my attacks. When she runs
a hot bath I can't tell whose skin she's
trying to burn. She won't believe me,

but the communism isn't the problem.
It's when she abandons me in an ocean
view room and I look out onto les galets,
when I see the yellow galaxy of umbrellas
along the *Promenade des Anglais,* when I
smell her ashtray overflowing on the table

de chevet, when I guess she's eating croque
madame alone at a café. That, or pissing in
a fountain and I know I'll get the call, then
I'll ring my father in Ohio and hear the creak
of his chair as he yells into the basement for
my brother, who is so heavy we are counting

the days until he will break through the stairs.
I ought to be ashamed. Instead, I take one step,
lowering myself down the ladder she left me.

THIS IS NOT A PIPE

That I should pity your multiple erections, poor
boy walking around with a crowbar in your pants.
One night I came home early from a late shift and
finally understood why Dad wouldn't discipline you—
he was naked in front of one of your favorite flicks.
Why couldn't you two keep your kiwis out of my face?
Mom gone, so every two weeks I scrubbed the house
of pubic hair. I wished I lived at the latest asylum.
You could not keep a job because you were always
calling in sleepy. You only left the house to pick up $40
Arby's orders. Who was watching me? Maybe I'm Miss
Remembering. I was always remodeling a condo
in my head. Misting the ferns with a mental mister.

SONG OF A MISANTHROPE

"Surely in isolation one becomes a god."
                    —William Carlos Williams

I've been reading too much into the
angels who dream of hurting me.

Take one pill with milk or food once a day.

I got your package in the mail.
Dishtowels and aprons.
Bruised fruit and volcanic rock.

Take four pills once a day.

I fight fringy impulses to dive
down flights of stairs, drink
household cleaning agents,
fondle hot surfaces and flames.

Take two pills three times a day.

Caution: may cause drowsiness,
throat pain, and in some rare cases,
acute angina. If you develop rash,
lightheadedness, or loss of life, please
call someone who gives a shit.

Take it all.

Here comes the prancy cat wearing
his white fur, bright orange swirls
like a frosty creamsicle. I will take
him into my arms, lick his creamy
forehead, his zesty stripes. I will
take one bite, feel the deep
freeze inside him.

LUNATIC YEARS

How quickly
    she became

a connoisseur
    of asylums.

We were left
    to practice

our more
    marketable forms

of suffering.
    Not once

did it occur
    to us to visit.

We all knew
    her forte

was white space.

HALLOWEEN IN THE TANK

All the hookers have spectacular stretch marks.

Not one of them will finger me for free.

It's how I learn that drinking is a bad hobby.

I ask the hookers which songs they wish were written for them.

They look like they're thinking pretty hard about that.

Outside, the world gloats over its children in drag.

INCOMMUNICADO

How does it start? I'm waiting for an oil change
and a smiling girl outside the glass is tap-

dancing in soccer cleats. I recall a photograph
of my mother from the year she broke all of our

contracts. She was wearing a light blue sweater
she knit herself, so the seams were loose. Always

in polyester pants, she seemed seduced by the
pleasure of scratching. It wasn't long after that

she disappeared. And for years all I knew of her
was a voice on the phone that was part goat.

She described shock treatments. Wait—did she
beg for them or beg off them? When the man calls

my name the girl is still tapping. Little shin guards.
She is making her mother laugh. He wants me to

spend $500 to fix a short. There are infinite reasons
I want to hurt him. I always only tried to give her

what she wanted.

After she disappeared from the last asylum I started
slowing at the bag lady's corner, seeking Mom's green
eyes. At home your 12-bar blues riffs grew so violent
the heat vents carried that shrilling up two floors.
Once a week the doctor admonished me for staying
sick. The table-paper splitting, he needled my pale
skin, the nurse fluttering close with the new spirometer.
That Christmas we were together in a car to cousin's.
Dad singing *Don't want ya, cause ya feets too big. Can't
use ya cause ya feets too big. I really hate ya cause ya feets
too big.* You ate a $75 platter of shrimp. Dad screamed,
I'm a better driver drunk than you ever will be sober.
When he passed out in the snow I grabbed his keys.

SONGS IN KISWAHILI

The flap unzips and I'm startled that we slept in the center
of a cloud. I find a snowbank, lift the bottle, and out splashes
1.5 liters of my overnight urine. In the mess we are force-fed:
our guide chanting *eat eat eat* and *drink drink drink*. The camp
team clanking pot after pot of steaming oatmeal and ginger tea.

I think of my brother guzzling Mountain Dew in the basement,
the windows blacked out with aluminum, the banister broken.
Once a week a hired girl does his shopping, stops at his favorite
restaurant for ten racks of ribs. Every morning he pads across
the rotting carpet, paws at his guitar, eats 7000 calories in bed.

I'm not sure I can stomach one more bite. Our guide repeats:
Eat this bread, drink this juice. I came all this way for the summit,
where we'll sing songs in Kiswahili, stop just shy of the vomit
spread out like fall leaves on the ice, sip Macallan 25 from a flask,
pose for more pictures than they took on the moon.

My guide gives me a plate of eggs, says, *you need this.* I nod.
But I *need* to take a shit. It's −10 degrees and I'm wearing seven
layers. I think of my brother's pendulous abdomen. He can't
climb the stairs to the bathroom so he goes in the sink where
our mother used to wash our cloth diapers. How does he wipe?

Then I eat until it hurts.

BREAK IN THE CHAIN

My friend Dana and I drove
        down Harrison Road to do Hands
               Across America. There was
a lot to look at out the car window.
      If it wasn't a hill it was green
              and if it wasn't green it was a curve.
The houses were ranch-style
        with long driveways and weeds
              sprouting out of the asphalt.
We always wanted long driveways
        but Dana and I lived in tract homes
             15 yards apart and our driveways
were made of 6 rectangular pads
      of concrete. Whenever a car came
             we looked at the antenna.
Some on the roof.
      Some near the windshield.
             Some near the trunk.
It was May 25, 1986.
      It was four months after my mother
             swallowed a bottle of pills.
Dana came to the hospital
      while they pumped
             my mother's stomach.
A car could be
      a bottle of pills. A car could be
             an antenna. A road could be
a curve. A hill could be green.
      A family could fall
             apart while holding hands
with 6.5 million people.
      How many of them are smiling?
             How many are receiving bad news?

FLATLINE

All summer it was not the dream
where the grooves of her skin
grayed, deepened. Not the dream

where she asked me for key lime pie.
Not the dream where her dog dipped
his curly head and drowned his peach

ear tips in a stale bowl. Not the
dream where the hot dove hovered
at the pool rim. Not the dream where

I found the dove in the
nest of her. This was the dream
where the earth went septic.

The heart started breaking all
its own records. It was the dream
where even the cocker spaniels

stood back from the equipment,
removed their blue masks,
snapped their latex gloves.

HOW I LEARNED THAT EVERYONE IS
RIDICULOUS

I was enjoying a long morning
of healthy rationalization.

It began with a memory of Barthes,
who once accosted me on my

way home from castration camp.
He accused me of being

all studium and no punctum.
Then he went on and on about

my lack of literary femininity.
Next Barth jumped in and said

I had mistaken the map for the city.
I argued that I am the message

in the bottle that floats all the way
from the Choptank to the Tagus.

He just shrugged and reminded me I was
born on the day that Abu Hasan farted.

Barthelme was kinder but not by much.
He promised that although he's tired of my

verbal pratfalls, he might absolve me
by tossing me over the balustrade

into the arms of Dan Rather's attacker(s).
You can see why I spent the rest of the afternoon

composing my personal eschatology.
It begins at a lectern where I am screaming,

LOOK BOYS, you can love your lover and your oeuvre
but only one of them will make you oeufs for breakfast.

Sometimes my apologies do more harm than good.

WHERE ARE YOU, GRAVITY?
—for Nick Flynn

This house is a frigate, a bridge for sale, a poker game, a firefly. It's a time warp, a time machine, a trap. It's worker's comp, rehab, restitution, order to re-convey. This house is a big sick lung. This house is a cave, a hovel, a hole. In this house we found everything that was lost. Two necklaces—one jade, one lapis; the land, the water. Shirt in a drawer for 35 years. This house is a 35-years drawer.

When he said, "You cannot come home." I said, "As you wish." I made a little house in my head. For 5 years, every phone call every letter. I pounded my chest. Gave 5 reasons why. Chanel N°5, size 5 shoes, 5 fingers, 5 toes, 5 little wishes. Five times with love or humility. Five times I left all I had on the begging table.

I'm arriving late for the party, the food half-eaten, the boxes over-turned. I hear my father shuffling a plastic shopping bag. I hear him coughing like the Stan Kenton Orchestra—strings, horns, percussion, brass. I try, but I can't hold my own breath as long as that cough.

Where are you, gravity? The first time I asked I was so pure that if you touched me I would shatter. The first time I asked he told me shock treatments, Thorazine, Lithium, restraints. The first time I asked, I wished I could be the bad child, the semi-conscious, the fat.

I wished I had never seen her thumb and its pulse. Her thumb like a snake's head, like a dying thing. Like a crooked branch, like a fidgeting foot. A thumb that wrestles itself. A thumb hitching a bad ride. A thumb being sucked. A thumb in the crack of the dam.

Where are you, gravity? When I tell my father never to die but he knows he is already dying? Packing to race to his deathbed feels like a goddamn Sharon Olds poem. The distance was the sanity in the first place. I wanted to open that door and find my mother and father at my age. I only ever wanted them to be my age.

Where are you, gravity? Where are you when the spinning-spasm starts? Where are you when the spinning-spasm ends?

At my father's funeral all the engineers
lined up to tell me they had been in love
with my mother. My wine glass kept
disappearing. The next day I returned
my black stiletto heels because *they hurt.*

When I knew her it was all about lithium.
I didn't even know where Palo Alto was.
Post-shock-treatment, her job was to fill
the bare backyard of our neo-colonial
with crab apple trellises, tomato plants,

but in college she studied German, drove a VW
up to the steps of Versailles, had an audience
with Pope John the 23RD at the Vatican, rode
Vespas with Spanish fascists. When she met
my father? She drove a convertible 911 and

loved to fuck. Who knew that in 10 years
she'd be shuttling me to asthma camp,
smoking with the windows shut. That my
brother would get so fat he would no longer
fit behind the steering wheel of his Honda

so he quit his job and never left the family
home again. That she and my father would
hate each other so much they couldn't bear their
cars sitting arms-distance apart in the garage.

LIMINAL

I don't need more of anything now. I don't need more to drink, I don't need more to read or to watch, no more to eat. I stand up from the dinner table and rub my son's head, kiss his blond hair. I smooth my daughter's ponytail, pat her on the shoulder and her eye catches my eye. We have not smiled at each other for years, I am thinking. In the kitchen, I run the water hot, hot enough to scrub soil from hands.

After work I like to watch the news, Channel 5, with the weatherman who bends at the knees. I like to read the Post. I pull the paper from its plastic bag then I peel the sections apart. I put the Front Page face-down on my legs. I cover it with the Local Daily, then I cover that with New Living. Sports and Classifieds go directly to the pile by the side of my chair. I watch the news, and I read the paper, and I don't get up until I can see my lap.

Last week I drove my Triumph TR8 off the side of the road. I can't remember leaving the bar. I didn't wake up until a farmer knocked on the window. He was wearing a hat that said "Lincoln, Nebraska." He drove me to his farmhouse and he called my wife.

I've had a recurring dream since I was a child. I'm standing on a tree stump that is 15 feet high. At first it is sturdy, and I am pleased because I can see for miles. I can see the store where my mother buys groceries. I can see the road that leads to my cousin's house, and the road that my father takes to work every day. I am standing on top of the tree stump, and I am straining to see all that I can see. But my desire turns fluid. My desire causes the stump to start swaying. Instead of creating vision, I have created motion. The stump sways left and so I lean right. The stump sways right and so I lean left.

And soon I've lost control. The stump falls down and I land on top of my house and my mother is dead.

Because the body is illiterate, lacks
language any more complex than *thirst;*
and because the body came from another
body whose ultimate goal was to wean it;
and because the body saw a body burst
into flames on the bow of a boat;
and because the body watched its dog cross
the uncrossable street about to be stopped by
the unstoppable car; and because the body
went from soft & pink to rough & brown;
and because the body feels a stabbing, a
tingling, a dull ache, a numbness, a heat;
and because the body would tell you this
if it could, would say *it hurts* or *I miss you.*

TAKE THE LATE FLIGHT

I am making a desert home
out of rainwater, brewing

the afternoon, constellating
furniture. I am going there

from here. When
I arrive you might drop

the sweating glass. Back
patio stray parades his sweet

choreography of mewing.
Last night the wind cooed

grapefruit straight off their boughs.
Look at the china bowl,

crystal shark's head, pocket
full of eyes. Look at

the mouse tit, leather hankie,
kaleidoscope of bones.

So what am I to do now?
Rearrange it, rearrange it.

You are the pewter pillow,
straw candle, tooth stone.

ON BEING ORPHANED

I find a shirt in my hand but can't remember
the word for shirt or hand. Or how to put it on?

Something about its four holes and my four limbs.
It's too colorful. It's too angular. Hold it up to the

light and it's too threadbare. It's a heap but somehow
it is supposed to encompass my body? Should I cut it,

then tie it back together? Or burn it and spread the ash?
I find a shirt in my hand but it might be a saucer

for my cup. It might be code for a special type of humor.
It might be music. Or an elephant's ear or a stingray.

I find a shirt in my hand and it could be political.
It could be asleep and will wake if I shake it. Will it

break if I drop it? Or will it bounce? I find a shirt
in my hand. I think my shadow should wear it.

AFTER RUMI'S BIRDWINGS
—*for Elizabyth*

Only a few months
off the sympathy dole,
I'm no longer the dying
child, bald on a ward.

My grief turned into the lost
year, long afternoons
stuck reading the same
sentence with still no sense

to be made of the jumble
of letters, and who made
letters anyway, how did
anyone curl them like tiny

hairs onto scraps of paper.
Now sadness is a sneeze.
It arrives during the punch line,
or when my mouth is full

of wishes. I'm wearing the joyful
face you've been wanting to see.

But then that tickle.

CRAVE

Will you at least watch the trees
until just after the swaying stops,

until the last leaves have fallen
into the great drain of the earth.

Ever since I was a child in your arms
see I am admitting it happened

you tried to place your finger
on the X of string that bows

into some small miracle.
At the ocean, when you were my age,

you mistook the sand for blossoms.
After sniffing fistfuls you screamed

So this is our fair universe.
I have promised others I will never

want the way you want.
They love me on this condition.

WHAT FLICKERS

October birthday candles
          make me long for January sex;
the clothes under the tuxedo.

That first winter we bought plenty
          of trinkets. It was the year of small
and mostly impotent accidents. It was

the year I exceled at the don't-eat-that diet.
          It was the year the cat came
out of her hiding place carrying

my list of impossible antidotes.
          Now we're stuck in the irrevocable
after. We've learned the pleasure

of summer coming down like an elbow,
          the pleasure of living alone
with money and her enzymes.

No one extra here to hate us.
          Everyone spends the day
doing some pointless thing.

Cat, you are a failure as a cat.

PERENNIAL

That was the year I had nothing but good
intentions. I ordered heirlooms from
the catalog. Amended the soil. Spring
arrived with its wardrobe of florals.
We had our fragrant days. Then everyone
died. First was my mother. On a bright
morning, planting peppers, packing mulch,
I got the coroner's call. Then I was hardly
into fall, just seeding the beets, and there
went my father. So I sowed. If you ask anyone
where I went that year they would tell you
to the garden. I did the digging with my
two hands. With my two bare hands.

RANK BITCH

That winter I became heir to a house the size of a stitch.

I woke to a dank room full of small and horrible consonants.

I woke longing for the dead, who would do me what good?

I woke in a ditch whose bank was a bloodbath of scrimshaw.

You and I stayed in love the way we always stayed in love.

We sat in those seats that stand up until you sit down.

I warned you that the movie was in French with no subtitles.

I warned you that angry girls cry with the gravitas of addicts.

You watched the film light flicker as if off the tines of a fork.

For me? You would ride the horse that just killed another horse.

You would hang my wedding garter from your rearview mirror.

That winter I woke trying to sing but my pitch stank.

I woke trying to solve the feel-better problem.

We are destined to grow old with the things that frighten us.

You are not a threat to me, except that you will die.

You, the dog who stares at my finger even when I point to the bone.

DAD'S LAST ENTRECHAT

We've entered
      a gentle collaboration.
You've agreed to be
      dead. I've agreed
to rewind your 30-
      year clock, its brass key
all cool and pre-recession.
      Later I'll realize
I don't know where I am.
      I am in a large car
somewhere between
      two geographical points.
Point A is known for
      its crying that sounds
like laughing. Point B
      has a river in the shape
of a noose. Now I
      can't imagine speaking
to a child with kindness.

CRUSHINGS

I haul yesterday's
garden trash

curbside, eye
the driver.

Will he glimpse
this dearth of petals?

Flagrant, rotten-
ripe, magenta.

Summer wears regret
like a blue apron.

From the porch
I watch the truck spasm,

its great flap closing.
I watch the things

I did not want
pressing hard against

all the things
no one else wanted.

BIZARRE PART

Today all I need
is this hammock,

some wind in the palms.
Tomorrow the oath

of a bell's hollow.
Next week the spot

on a doe.
I promised that you

wouldn't appear in these poems.
But only you can answer,

what makes a life a good life?
And if, after dreaming, I wake to find

this earth unchanged by the dream,
only you can answer,

how do I tell the difference?

ON BEING BORN

"the letters of my name are written under the lids
of the newborn child."

—Adrienne Rich

Yesterday I thought I found
my own bones in a fossil rock.

In the womb I was a wheel.
Head chasing feet, I beat

my mother into dizzy fits
so that after I was born

she never felt full again.
My mother took

her birthday and ran.
In the womb she was

some kind of stone.
The only daughter

of an only daughter,
as I am an only daughter.

I have their hips now,
their delicate ankles,

their feet the size of hands.
I am wearing the name

they gave me,
last nesting doll.

CLIMBING

This fog is my own private cloud.
The goggles steam as if my eyes can breathe.

I remove them, risk blindness. I feel the top.
I want to reach it with eyes as well as feet.

I am so winded the whipping
oranges, blues, reds of the prayer flags

sound like whispers compared to the two
new beating hearts I wear as earmuffs.

Descending, the snow gets heavier,
the white closing in like milk

covering the cat's tongue.
Without warning I am sliding

into its fat, black mouth.
I am plummeting down the ravine

behind my childhood home.
I am living the dream of pillars.

I am landing the axe
to save myself.

NOT HAVING THEM

Yesterday's rain was finally level
headed. Light depressions pocked
the pool like mice crossing the water.

Usually it starts as a murmur and grows
to a hum. Gutters flood. Trees hang heads
as if accepting criticisms veiled as compliments.

Today I am thinking about all those cigarettes.
Did they smoke to help us?
Or did they know we would help them

while they took turns with their melodious
dying. Our mother, smoldering.
What else would she have to give up?

I've asked nothing of my children, besides
not having them out of fear I would ask too much.
Today the rain is in between falling hard

and falling short. Either way, it extinguishes
all the small desires of my life.

THE LINGER MUSEUM

I spend all day in a room
with every item I will ever own.

Along one wall I'm touching wooden birds
that I've mistaken as soft. Look in that corner:

the fishes, who have their own needs.
On a high shelf, there's a tree that has

a melody in mind. Up ahead:
two cars big enough for ceiling fans.

By noon I'm reaching out to touch
my father: he is holding a spoon over-hand.

There is the dog I loved despite his dog-ness!
There is the gentler woman I once was.

Look! There's my mother freaking
out in public. I think, am I still here?

And if so, how much will that cost me?
When evening falls I'm busy fitting

babies back into wombs.

MY TRIFECTA OF OFFENSES

The neighbors tsk when I drive
my riding mower to the liquor store.

They stand on their lawns blowing
smoke out of their bird-mouths.

They're mad at me for blatantly
losing both my parents in a year.

See them lounging in egregious chairs.
Their dog-on-a-chain barks like he's been

asked to choose which fire will engulf him.
At least my motor means I'm *somewhere*.

I give them the prize-float wave then fade
into the darkness that leaks from trees.

WITH A WHIMPER

First I look at some Eliot, which puts me
straight to sleep for a lovely hour or so.
I just can't do it. What a prig. But I'm glad I try.

Since it's hard, I decide to write one of those
poems that gets by on a few clever ploys.
It starts with a dream that I'll try to pass off

as not a dream. I'm stealing a Danish and eating it
in a parking lot while dodging cars driven
by nonagenarians who remind me of my parents.

Shit. Everything reminds me of them.
Like trying to read Eliot, blah blah blah,
and all I can think of is Mom and Dad in urns.

Then I see a man with his small son.
I see a tender look between them. That hurts
like hell. But I don't even need that image.

Just say *man* or *son*. Just say *woman* or *daughter*.
Doctor put me on the stare-pills.
I can't feel my distal parts.

Yesterday I invented fire.
Today I'm hemming flames.

ACKNOWLEDGMENTS

My sincere gratitude to the editors of the following literary magazines where these poems first appeared, sometimes in previous versions.

The Adirondack Review	"After Rumi's Birdwings"
The American Poetry Review	"Night Falling, Czechoslovakia" and "Letter from the Psych Ward, Hospital Kashenko"
Arcadia Magazine	"Songs in Kiswahili"
Armchair/Shotgun	"XVIIIE Arrondissement"
The Baltimore Review	"Dad's Last Entrechat"
Belleview Literary Review	"Reading Sexton in Phuket"
Bluestem Magazine	"Cutlass Ciera"
Burnside Review	"Murmur"
Cimarron Review	"On Being Born"
Cleaver	"The Birth of No"
Cobalt Review	"Losing Our Milk Teeth"
Cutbank	"Flatline" and "Liminal"
Diode	"Arch on a Rung" and "Edison's Medicine"
A Dozen Nothing	"Everyone Is Eviscerated"
Evansville Review	"Not Having Them"
The Greensboro Review	"Lunatic Years"
Gulf Coast	"Why I Burned Down Namdaemun Gate"
Hobart	"Scrotum and Bone" and "Bulb"
Kalliope	"How the Body Moves"
The Madison Review	"The Princess of Creeping," "What Flickers," and "The Linger Museum"
The Massachusetts Review	"Crave"
Natural Bridge	"Perennial"
Nebraska Review	"Song of a Misanthrope" and "Take the Late Flight"
NewSouth	"Crushings"
North American Review	"Rank Bitch"
Prick of the Spindle	"Where Are You, Gravity?"
Quarterly West	"Is It the Sea You Hear in Me?"
Seattle Review	"My Brother, Hoarding"
Sixth Finch	"Halloween in the Tank"
Smartish Pace	"My Trifecta of Offenses"
South Dakota Review	"Climbing"
Third Coast	"Throwing the Proper Tantrums" and "Midnight at Orca Cannery"

"Why I Burned Down Namdaemun Gate" won the 2009 *Gulf Coast* Prize for Poetry judged by Brigit Pegeen Kelly.

"After Rumi's Birdwings" was a finalist for the 2011 46er Poetry Prize at *The Adirondack Review.*

"The Linger Museum" and "What Flickers" won the 2012 Phyllis Smart-Young Poetry Prize from *The Madison Review.*

"Reading Sexton in Phuket" won Honorable Mention for the 2013 Marcia and Jan Vilcek Prize for Poetry at *Bellevue Literary Review* selected by Mark Doty.

"Rank Bitch" was a finalist for the 2013 James Hearst Poetry Prize at the *North American Review.*

"Losing Our Milk Teeth," "Feeding Peeping Tom," and "Good Morning, Mediocrity" were finalists for the *Cobalt Review* Poetry Prize 2013.

"My Trifecta of Offenses" was a finalist in the 2013 Beullah Rose Poetry Prize at *Smartish Pace.*

"Midnight at Orca Cannery" was a finalist in the *Third Coast* Poetry Prize 2014.

"Incommunicado" was a finalist for the *Yemasssee* Poetry Prize in 2014.

My deepest thanks to Stephen Dunn, who chose this manuscript for the 2016 May Swenson Poetry Award. Thanks to Michael Spooner and Allie Madden at USUP. Thank you to my Ten Poems Group, who read many of these pieces in their earliest stages: Pete Miller, Elizabyth Hiscox, Sarah Pape, Alex Linden, Robert Krut, Todd Robinson, Maureen Alsop, Brenda Sieczkowski. Thanks to my early teachers who continue to bless me with support and love: Irene O'Connor, Diane Parsons, Joyce Yonka, and Mary Hennigan. Thanks to my ASU support: Beckian, Jeannine, Norman, Tito, Cynthia, and the fabulous Karla Elling. Thanks for safe harbor where I wrote many of these poems: Vermont Studio Center, Atlantic Center for the Arts, Mesa Refuge, and Ragdale Foundation. Thanks to the many people who commented on this work along the way: Nick Flynn, Gregory Orr, Ray Gonzalez, Terese Svoboda, Natasha Tretheway, Mark Yakich, Josh Rathkamp, Judith Van, Shannon Camlin Ward, Rae Gouirand, Alice Jones, Hayley Larson, and Amy Lerman. Thanks to all of my family in its un-hemmable glory. And more, thanks to John for helping me hem innumerable flames.

Patricia Colleen Murphy founded *Superstition Review* at Arizona State University, where she teaches creative writing and magazine production. Her writing has appeared in many literary journals, including *The Iowa Review*, *Quarterly West*, and *American Poetry Review*, and most recently in *North American Review*, *Smartish Pace*, *Burnside Review*, *Poetry Northwest*, *Third Coast*, *Hobart*, *decomP*, *Midway Journal*, *Armchair/Shotgun*, and *Natural Bridge*. Her work has received awards from the Associated Writing Programs and the Academy of American Poets, Gulf Coast, *Bellevue Literary Review*, *The Madison Review*, Glimmer Train Press, and *The Southern California Review*. A chapter of her memoir-in-progress was published as a chapbook by *New Orleans Review*. She reviews literary magazines at Lit Mag Lunch and books on Goodreads. She lives in Phoenix, AZ.